WE WON DIDN'T WE SARGE?

Poetry by LCpl 777

Peter Smith

citizenpete@yahoo.com

Copyright © 2020 Peter Smith (citizenpete@yahoo.com)

All rights reserved

The characters and events portrayed in this book are fictitious. Any similarity to real persons, living or dead, is coincidental and not intended by the author.

No part of this book may be reproduced, or stored in a retrieval system, or transmitted in any form or by any means, electronic, mechanical, photocopying, recording, or otherwise, without express written permission of the publisher.

ISBN: 9798512271230

Cover design by: Art Painter
Library of Congress Control Number: 2018675309
Printed in the United States of America

Dedicated to alll members of our Emergency Service, Armed Forces and Veterans.

May you continue to be amazing.

And my family x

CONTENTS

Title Page
Copyright
Dedication
A hug for the future   1
Don't panic   2
Kicking Leaves   4
Now is the time.   6
The last pint.   8
MY BLIND FAITH   9
Summer 2020   11
Ooops   13
My town.   15
A Protest   17
It's okay   18
I found a magic wand!   19
Some days   20
Leaving   21
Don't listen to me   22
OH, it's election day again.   23
Far, far away.   24
We won didn't we Sarge?   25

Flip Flop	28
There's a politician on the doorstep dad!	30
The Telly Cop	32
The Form	33
Mad Crowd Disease	35
Love	36
Oh bugger	38
A Promise	39
I choose	40
History!	42
The irrelevance of time.	43
Keep your hands off my beer	45
Just a moment	46
Gullumphing	47
Sit	48
Maserati	49
No picture	50
Cat-or-rise-ation	51
The Moon	52
Face Book	54
Tree Tops	55
Shouting	56
Cog	57
Merry Christmas	58
Two points	60
Nothing lasts forever	61
A little kinder	62
World's still here	63

Beast	64
Christmas is coming	66
Travellers	67
My Icicle	68
Too Much Irony to Do	69
The Star of the Show	71
Hold your Horses	73
A quick release	75
The News	76
The Internet Guru	79
A mirror	80
Sunrise	82
CHANNEL SURFING	84

A HUG FOR THE FUTURE

Today I made a difference.
It wasn't very much.
I simply stayed away
I couldn't even touch.

I did not shake your hand
Nor give you a big hug
I had to stand a way away
So I wouldn't pass the bug.

No pat upon the back to give
Nor nudge upon the shoulder
But that's so we can both still live
I'll hug you when we're older.

DON'T PANIC

Don't panic when the bombs are dropping,
They're not dropping on us.
Don't panic when the homeless are dying
That's nothing to do with us.

We're all warm and cosy
In our lovely house.
While the emergency services
Are out and about.

Don't panic when a baby's crying
It's not our child.
Don't panic for our ordered life
Has not gone wild.

Oh dear, I hear our neighbours got a cough,
Panic! Get to the shop right now.
Buy. Panic. Put your nose in the trough.
Eat a tiny piece of the real fear, pow!

Don't panic now.
It's too late.
Don't panic ?

There's no loo roll, rice or flour
On the shelf.

Everyone is grabbing
Everything for themself.

No tins of toms or beans to see
No bread left for the key workers
Nor any for the family and me.

Oh, Wait! Panic...

KICKING LEAVES

Today is just another day.
But tomorrow holds every possible way,
Maybe it will be just another day.
Or maybe it won't!

Maybe tomorrow you'll find love
In a world you never saw before,
Maybe you'll meet an old friend,
That you've never seen and will see once more.

Maybe in the rain and wind
You'll find a freedom alone,
That you dreamt of as a child
But now your grown up you can go wild.

Kick leaves,
Laugh,
Smile,
Don't have a bath!
Ignore grown ups!

Tomorrow is the great unknown.
We all face tomorrow
But not alone.
Remember that.
We are never alone.

Unless we live on an island,
Which few of us do.
But but those that do
Still have to acknowledge
Me and you.
(Get out of that without moving!)

Maybe you'll just have a cup of tea
And a cosy biscuit or two?
For tomorrow
Is entirely up to you.

As for me,
You'll find me kicking leaves
Or wondering how to climb a tree,
At my age!
If I call you.
Bloody well answer,
Because I might actually be stuck up a tree!

Whatever you do tomorrow
Starts with today.
And today is just another day.
Every day is a good day.
Bring on tomorrow.

NOW IS THE TIME.

What have we done now!
Arrogance and ignorance
Has brought us to this place.
Now we must learn
To keep our space.

Now is the time to be your best.
Now is your time to shine.
Now is the time to take advice
From those who know better
With minds wiser than mine.

Now is the time
To be that hero
That movie star.
We are real and we are who we are.
Not some fictional character on a screen.

We are the people who will live through this
For real.

Now is the time for crayons
For the kids to bake and
For us to take stock
And realise what really matters.

Food for the needy
Respect for a law which keeps
Each one of us
As safe as we can be.

Now is the time
To knock on a neighbour's door.
And make sure they are okay.

We don't need to swing from helicopters
Or run through burning buildings
To be a hero
For our children, our families,
Our communities.

Now is the time to do small things.
But small things that matter.
Not for praise or recognition.
For our community
For our families
For our future.

Now is our time to act!
And act we must!

THE LAST PINT.

The shelves are looking empty
The stocks are running low.
We're told we have to stay at home.
So where do the homeless go?

No more pints a pouring
Until further notice is given
If you've decided to start panicking
You may not be forgiven.

Keeping calm and getting by
Is the mantra we all hear.
But across the land
The British shout

But what about our beer!

MY BLIND FAITH

I've got myself a new detergent pack,
With a crystal clear lake on the back,
It goes with my new Zanussi,
Sold to me by my friend on TV.

He really is a nice man,
And he does all he can,
To make my days better,
In his red and green sweater.

And the woman who looks so nice,
Fills up my life with spice,
So I buy the gravy she does,
And chocolates because that's what she loves.

While my weekly contribution,
To the hidden tax institution,
Means I might be a little richer,
By the time Sunday hits the picture.

So soon I'll be on cable,
And old Big Brother will then be able,
To sell me two way tele-scan,
Then I'll be visible to the man,

Who sells me all the dreams I need,

PETER JAMES SMITH

In riding garb and country tweed,
My friends the people on TV.
They really care for me.

And I know all about the subversive bad,
'Cause there's a documentary we had,
And then a programme to let me see,
They wouldn't let them lie to me.

So from the moment I arise,
With the Breakfast News before my eyes,
I spend my days with the ad men who care,
It's far much safer than to go out there.

For that world is not a nice place to be,
I know, I've seen it on my TV,
So here in my front room I'm safe,
Just Me, My TV and My Blinding Faith.

SUMMER 2020

Coming out of lock down
The Hot and sweaty penguins
Are heading to the beech.

Dressed in shorts and T-shirts
Swimsuits and surgical masks.
No where to use the toilet
None open for a pee.
So the hot and sweaty penguins are pissing in the sea.

They're climbing into gardens
To drop a little poo
And the council officials
Really don't know what to do.

The rubbish is piling high
Thirty five tonnes left on the beach
As only one day goes by
The penguins are now at home out of reach.

They'll be back again tomorrow
Yet the virus is not gone.
The hot and sweaty penguins
Cannot see what they've done wrong.

In queues that stream with hips to hips.
They'll push their masks upon their head
As they eat their take away fish and chips.
The scientists watch these scenes with dread.

They are warning and warning

PETER JAMES SMITH

How the virus is spread but what can they do.
Inform the penguins in the morning
We might be going into lock down two!

OOOPS

If I stumbled
Would you help me up?
If I failed
Could you help me win.

If I lost everything
Should I begin again.
Tell me friend
Would you be there?

Tell me friend
Could you care?
If we pass but do not see
If we see but do not hear
What worth is either
In a world without care.

Suddenly we do care
Suddenly we see
The value of each other
And all humanity.

If you stumble
I'll help you up.
If you fail
I'll help you succeed.

PETER JAMES SMITH

Who am I?
Why I'm the voice inside your head.
I'm everything you have ever done
And everything you've said.

You've come this far
With tales to tell
Those sagas I wait to hear again.
So stay strong
Stay you

Until we sit by the fire and long stories are told
Of days gone by
The young and old
Stay strong.

MY TOWN.

I love my town
And the people in it.

We keep our distance.
We keep safe.
We look after each other.
We follow the rules.

Even though we are a town more full of individuals and rebels
Than you could ever wish to meet.

You could never meet
So many wonderful people in one place.
We keep our space.
To protect our town,
Our NHS.
Our country.

We keep our discussions distant on the street.

We care and between us
We do know everyone.
We will look after our own.

Even the pains in the preverbial!
But they are our pains
And they are

PETER JAMES SMITH

Our people.

Stay strong my wonderful world of Mere.
If I'm to face 'the end of the world as we know it'
Then I'm happy to face it here.
No better company would I request.
I've shared it for twenty years no less.

But if you don't come from here.
Don't get in your car and come here.
It's not that we don't like you.
It's just we love our loved ones more.

Come visit when the dark clouds have passed.
You'll find enough nutters down the pub
To entertain you for a lifetime!
Especially on the day they reopen!

I'll be at the front of the queue.

A PROTEST

We're having a protest
To say we won't be told what to do.
Managed to get a slot booked
From ten till two.

Next Saturday but one.

We did want it on a different day
But that's the only day
We were allowed that week.

But hey,
We're having a protest anyway.
Next Saturday but one
From ten till two.

IT'S OKAY

We're taking over the world today.
It's okay.
Nothing will change.
Our promises like dust
Though cast in iron
Will rust.

We're going to make sure
We stay rich
And you
Stay poor.

Though obviously we'll get clever chaps
To gloss over our mishaps
To keep the status quo.

I FOUND A MAGIC WAND!

I found a magic wand today
Just lying on the floor.
I found a magic wand today
I'm not sure what it's for?

Maybe the trees are talking.
The birds sing oh so loud.
I found a magic wand today
Missed by the busy crowd.

I suppose I'll just keep hold of it
Until I meet someone magical
Who may or may not need it.
A magic wand how fantasmagorical!

SOME DAYS

Some days just turn off your phone.
Walk out the door
And go on an adventure
Without anyone else.

Visit a shop which you like.
Grab an old bike and ride.
Take a walk to the countryside.
Leave the phone on the shelf.

Some days it's goo
To just be yourself

LEAVING

I decided to leave the world today.
Alas nobody noticed.
So I left.
And they all carried on!
I came back tomorrow
And they didn't even notice I
Was gone

I suppose I'll carry on
Regardless.

DON'T LISTEN TO ME

Do not go blindly if you have eyes to see
Do not fear if you have ears to hear.
Don't listen to me.
I'm deaf, half blind and free.
Do not, at all costs, listen to me x

History!

Understand it.
Learn from it.
And take in the view.
Because
History
Is
Me and
You.

OH, IT'S ELECTION DAY AGAIN.

Here comes that rarely seen creature.
A knocking at my door.
To make the same old promises
I've heard a hundred times before.
To look after the young, the elderly, the poor.
If I'll only vote for them
Who've never seen me before.

Keep their promises?
They never ever will.
But half the country will vote for them still.
Bloody politicians,
Once every five years,
It's like trick or treat,
All over again.

We're all just little human beings
Trying to make our way.
There are the bad ones
Which we learn to avoid.
Some learn the easy way.
Some learn the hard way.
But at the end of the day
We're all just little human beings anyway.

FAR, FAR AWAY.

That's where I want to be.
But even far far away,
I'll still be with me.

Far, far away is here.
Far from the madness
War and fear.
Far, far away is really near.

I like far, far away.
I think I'll stay here.

WE WON DIDN'T WE SARGE?

That's it lad, you can go home now
The fightings done and we won.

It doesn't feel like we won Sarge
What with so many young men and women dead.
So many lives ruined.

No lad, it doesn't
But we survived, so we won.

What'll I do now Sarge?

You'll be fine lad
They're making a land fit for heroes back home.
They'll take care of you.

But Sarge, my mind's a mess and my body sore
I really don't know who I am any more
How will I survive the peace?

Don't you worry lad
You've done your duty
They'll look after you.

Hello Sarge it's been a few years
We've shed a few tears
And time has passed,

PETER JAMES SMITH

But we're still here eh Sarge
We won.

How you keeping lad?
Did they keep their promises
As you kept yours
Fighting in their wars?

No Sarge, I sleep rough on the street
And my mental health isn't good.
I have to beg for help
But you know Sarge, I don't like to.
But we won though, didn't we Sarge
Just they forgot to build a land fit for heroes.

Aye lad, we won.
Here's five pounds
Go get yourself a coffee lad.
There's no more I can do.
Since I got back home
I've been just the same as you.

But we'll get through it won't we Sarge

Of course lad, we always do.
We have to
We owe it to our fallen comrades.
They may forget us and the promises made
Leaving our heroes on the street.

But we never forget, Sarge.

No lad. We never forget.

FLIP FLOP

A flip flop.

A Care Bear.
A small pushchair.
A book of words.
A dream or two.

Be careful as you walk on through.

A blanket.
Some toys.
No noise now.
Just dust.

This building will never last long enough to rust.

A cot.
A playpen.
A chart taped to the wall
to tell when to go to school and the dreams to keep.

When you are safely tucked up in your sleep.

More dust.

A sight.
A hand.
A sock.
Shock.

A child.

Another.
Sister and brother.
No dreams to dream anymore.
Who do you carry out first?

And what do you carry out last?

A question I believe that most
Would dread to ask.
Is there a future to their past?
These children lay dead on the floor everyday.

And if we are a civilized world it shouldn't be that way!

A shell hole
In the wall.
Seems to be
Quite no big news at all.

Tell that to the man who has to carry out
These tiny bodies to the parents
Who are waiting
In the rubble outside their home.

Alone.

THERE'S A POLITICIAN ON
THE DOORSTEP DAD!

Hello,
I am a politician as you can plainly see.
I promise that I'll care for you
If you'll only vote for me.

Sorry that we didn't care before
That's someone else's fault.
But this time we'll get it right
Just give me the keys to the vault.

I'll spend much more on health care
And education too.
Well for my family and my other politicians
Obviously not you.

It's sad you've had to struggle
But really, say no more.
I am a politician
A standing at your door.

I'll not bore you now
With policies and other kinds of dross
But when you see my name
Could you simply put a cross.

A fair request I thought myself
And I'm happy to oblige
I now have fifteen crosses
In the field just outside.

THE TELLY COP

Rice, Rice, store in a cool dry place.
The burning red of a rocket trace.
Myths of beauty on a models face.
As the telly cop opens another case.

Actually reality is nearly here
As virtual reproductions come quiet near.
Rivers of blood run crystal clear
While the populous is kept in line by fear.

Orchestrated options so cleverly sublime
Another law comes out in time
Corruption is no longer classed as crime
Protesting voices may as well be mime.

Everything's for sale, it's one big shop.
The band wagon is big and on we all hop.
There seems no way to make the madness stop.
As another case closes for the telly cop.

THE FORM

We all want to change the world, apparently.
I've found the best way
Is day by day
And bit by bit.
Everyday
The world just gets that
Little
Bit
Better
If you bother
To make it that way.

Until...the system:

Hello, I've filled in the form, there you go.
Are there any gaps sir?
Gaps?
In your history, are there any gaps?
And by gap you mean?
Gaps, gaps in time and space that cannot be accounted for, gaps!
Oh yes, there are many gaps.
And what were you doing during these gaps?!
Well, I'm not sure because by your definition, and I have to agree, also mine, they are places in time and space that cannot be accounted for.
Gaps?

PETER JAMES SMITH

Gaps.
I'm off to fill in the gaps.

Tomorrow

MAD CROWD DISEASE

I'm staying in to avoid
'Mad Crowd Disease'!
It's spreading faster
Than any other virus
On the planet!

LOVE

Love doesn't come out of a packet,
You can't buy it in a shop.
Love doesn't come out of pretending to be
Something that you're not.

Love can't be bought or traded
It doesn't work that way.
Love is something you find
Along the way.

Love cannot be demanded
Love cannot be ordered or called.

Love will find you
When you are ready to give love
Until that day
Love
May mean nothing at all.

Ah, but when you find it
It's all the jewels that you may ever see.
For love and life and knowledge,
Is all you'll ever be.

Take those three
And pass them on.

And love will continue
Long after we are gone.

OH BUGGER

Is it the end of the world again?

I reckon I must have lived through
at least twenty 'end of the worlds'.

I have to say,
it gets a bit boring
In the end.

And the world?

In the end?

It seems to be still here. x

But different.

This time.

Very different!

A PROMISE

A promise is a promise
And comes with such a cost.
For if you break a promise
Then my friend you word is lost.

Your word in truth
Is all you have
To keep or throw away.
But your word defines you
To the world
Each and everyday.

I CHOOSE

I choose happiness
Over sadness.
I choose truth
Over lies.
I choose strength
Over weakness
Though often I cries.

I make mistakes
I get things wrong
I'm not perfect
I have faults.
My demons I keeps locked away
In hidden secret vaults.

My children are grown
And happy
My bank account is poor
But I wouldn't choose
It differently
I know what life is for.

It's choices we all have to make.
On our choices things depend.
And the choices that we've made.
Makes you and me my friend.

So for all the tea in China
Or the diamonds in the sand.
I choose this life
For happiness.
Though most of it unplanned.

I'm sure you'll understand.

HISTORY!

Understand it.

Learn from it.

And take in the view.

Because

History

Is

Me and

You.

THE IRRELEVANCE OF TIME.

An hour ago yesterday
Isn't an hour ago today.
An hour to come
Has yet to be.

But that hour, once eleven
Not Ten
Or was it twelve?
Whatever, it won't come again.

It will be that this weekly cycle will repeat.
Sunday will come again.
But although the name matches
It just won't be the same.

The clocks go forward
The clocks go back.
The pages on the calendar turn.
The same days and months pass by.

But do we ever learn?
The same mistakes, heartbreaks and joys.
The same old song is heard
From the blackbird or nightingale.

I have in mind

There is an irrelevance
In
Time.

The moment is where we all live for sure.
The imagination makes for us the moment endure.
Better times to come we dream.
But right here, right now, we float
In the stream of imagined time.

Life is only a moment long
Memory a strand of moments.
Every moment is precious and precise.
So don't waste time believing in time.

Nobody knows what is to come.

For time in itself is irrelevant.

There is no time. Only now.

KEEP YOUR HANDS OFF MY BEER

Everyone seems to want to know what's going on,
They don't.
Everyone thinks they can change what's wrong,
They won't.

Everyone thinks that they are right,
They're not.
Everyone thinks they won't be forgot,
They will.

Everyone thinks they're bullet proof,
Until they get shot.
Everyone wants to live forever,
They will not.

Be happy, be sad.
Laugh and cry the same.
For whatever anyone thinks,
Life is a crazy little game.

No person is any more or less to me.
Regardless of their religion, status or ability.
Each to their own for this jolly jape we call life.
Just keep your hands off my children, my beer and my wife. ;-)

JUST A MOMENT

For one brief moment on a tiny ball in space,
We shine, for one brief moment.
For one brief moment we are conscious energy,
Made form but only for a moment.

A lifetime is a moment and a moment is a lifetime.
For one brief moment let yourself enjoy
This one brief moment.

It's all we've got and it's all we get.
What and why I cannot know or say.
But for one brief moment
Why not love it anyway.

GULLUMPHING

Gullumphing, we shall not go
Until the season that brings us snow.
So bridlestitch and brandy snap
The summer all day long
For foggy morn and snifflepitch
Shall be here afore to long

Then we'll quimble and braerly moan
The winter each night gone
Of how we should have quival shaked
The summer all night long.

SIT

If you would like to sit with me for a day, I could tell you about my life.

If you would like to sit with me for a day, you could tell me about your life.

Or we could just sit quietly and think about our own lives.

Or we could just sit quietly and think about life.

Or we could just sit quietly.

Or we could just sit.

Or we could just be.

Maybe?

MASERATI

I don't need a Maserati,
To take me to a party.
I need to dance until dawn.
With my eyes closed.

Open them wide at sunlight.
See a thousand souls dancing bright.
I need don't need a Maserati,
To take me to a party tonight.

I need a fleet of buses.
And then more room.
Let's dance.
Begone this prophet of doom.

While we have music and love and romance.

Let's leg it before the bar bill arrives.

And dance...

NO PICTURE

Oops I forgot to take a picture of my amazing life,
Forgot to take a picture of my amazing children and wife.

Forgot to take a picture of my amazing me.

You'll just have to make do with some poetry. xx

CAT-OR-RISE-ATION

Do I have a category, I feel I'm missing out!
I'm not transgender, gay or bi,
What is this all about?

I'm not a particular colour, though I'd say I'm rather light.
I've relatives of many shades and none of them look white.

So take away the colour, the religion and the greed.
What am I to me and those I see,
If not a label, a ticket, a care.
What am I if I see you but to you
I'm not really there.

Just a side line to your magnificence,
Just a listener to your song?
What was I born for?
What is the point?

THE MOON

I went to the moon on a rocket ship made from a plastic bottle piloted by a man made from a wooden spoon.

I learnt jibberish from two chaps made of flower pots and a Dandelion that had a name. I heard a hand full of songs and laughed at zippy,

I had Itzy and Bitzy but they both looked the same to me.

And every time I get in a lift I make the sound of Mary, Mungo and Midge quietly in my head, free.

And Hartley the Hare and Toppove the monkey are still talking to a pig with a Brummie accent.

And then I grew up....Apparently!

Now I have the leaders of the known world to listen to and they make far less sense to me.

They talk more shit and do far less to make me think the world is a better and safer place.

Bring back Bungle, bring back George, Bring back some joy!!!

Bring back some Hope!!!

Bring back Rainbow!

And let's get on with loving the silly and simple things in life.

That's how to beat this fear!

Bring back you being near.

(not too soon obviously!)

So I say watch a silly movie, dance in the rain, tell someone you love them, never be ashamed to be just normal.

But normal, don't forget, is great.

Normal men and women have laid down their lives, their hopes, their fairy tales and their dreams to make their children, their grandchildren and you safe and happy.

If we let this go, in a swirl of electronic rubbish, then I say No.

Switch off the machine, look at the humans around you and love them.

Be normal, before we forget what normal is.

The future maybe coming but it is not decided yet.

Many brave souls are fighting yet.

And they are just normal.

Like me and you.

...(oh and I'm not sure but I don't think I'm normal after all) xxx

FACE BOOK

Oh my lord I have a problem with my Facebook stream.
It seems they know what I had for Sunday dinner.
And also, where I've been.

They know how old my kids are and how long I've been married to my wife.
In fact it's almost as if they know everything about my life!

I wonder how they managed to know every thing about me.
And then I remembers I gave them all my personal information free. ;-)

TREE TOPS

Today is cold misty.

On days like this I miss my knee length shorts and shabby jumper.

On days like this long ago trees were for climbing, no leaves to hide the way.

Alas I will stay earth bound today.

Yet I can still see that boy at the top of the tree.

Because I am that boy and that boy is me.

SHOUTING

Hey! People keep shouting and seem like they need to be heard.

I feel the same so I'm having a word.

I walk through this mad and crazy life with a simple philosophy.

I am what I am and as far as I am able I am one of the good guys who sits at this table called life.

I'm not cool or trendy.

I'm not rich or successful in other people's measuring lens.

But I have a wonderful family and some wonderful friends.

The hard times may come but I face them in knowing,

that no matter how hard there's no bad seeds that I'm sowing.

And when I check my balance sheet as I go to bed at night, it generally reads "I'm alright." ;-)

So shout if you must but talking is stronger.

Listen as well it just might take longer to hear all the voices of those who complain.

But remember that many are not really in pain.

Those who shout loudest are generally heard but from those with no voice you don't hear a word.

Use the intelligence that you think you have to be more than you're expected to be, and at the end of the day don't listen to me. Xxx

COG

You can only know what it is like to be a cog, when you have been a cog.

The size of the machine does not count because every cog counts.

From the tiniest wheel to the biggest of engines every cog counts.

A cog is an amazing thing to be.
So be a cog, choose the right machine, I'm sure you know what I mean.

Be a great cog.
Be a small part of the big machine. machine.
Be the machine.

Steer it and remember that every cog is the captain of their own destiny.

What a ship we could sail in if we built the machine with all the cogs in the right place?

MERRY CHRISTMAS

The good ones keep on being good, and the bad ones stay the same.

The lovers keep on watching stars and remembering their names.

The rich just keep on being rich and the poor keep being poor.

And the ones in the middle feel squeezed and certainly unsure.

The charitable keep giving and the selfish never do.

It doesn't matter who they are, it matters who are you.

Look not this year what others have or even what they do, you'll end up being dissatisfied that certainly is true.

This Christmas time remember the memories you make, are for the ones you love and all who see that you are not fake.

Be genuine and who you are this time and all the year.

And you will not need just Christmas time to be happy and full of cheer.

Do not fear your path if you are honest, kind and true.

And remember that though you can't see yourself
everyone else can see you too.

Merry Christmas and a prosperous New Year.

TWO POINTS

You have two definite points in life over which you have no control.

The day you are born and the day you die.
In between it is up to you who you are.
You alone decide.
Nobody else.

It does not matter what others chose to do.
That is them not you.
You are the power in your life.
You are your life.

Live it and love it...and be the best you can be for you and all those around you.

And when it's over know that you were the best of humanity. Xxx

NOTHING LASTS FOREVER

The world is always ending.

And always beginning.

The truth is our world is what we choose to make it.

Less can be made more or more can be made less.

It really is just a matter of how you see it.

Listen to yourself and you will have the wisest of councils.

We are spirits of the universe, here for the blink of an eye and then gone.

Do not let others distract you or you will blink and it will be gone before you end this moment and travel on.

Nobody here will last forever in this form but your energy and spirit will go to whichever next place awaits.

Our lack of understanding makes us question too much and listen to others that really know no more than we do.

Believe in yourself and believe in the universe and believe that it is what it is and has no name.

Take what you need, give what you can and be the best you can be, always and every day.

Then poor or rich, famous or obscure, true happiness will come your way.

A LITTLE KINDER

Why not try this tomorrow:

Walk a little slower, look around a little more, think a little deeper about what your life is for.

Be a little kinder with everyone you meet today and realise it's the little things you do that go a long long way

WORLD'S STILL HERE

Went to work today.

World hadn't ended.

All the people were still the same.

Went to the shop, still the same.

Walked home, still the same.

Sun shone, rain fell.

Still the same.

For anyone still in their bunker, don't worry, it is all still the same our here.

BEAST

There is a beast that roams our lands
Unseen yet deadly.
It is indifferent to your status
Your race or your religion.

The beast may live upon anyone.
It has no care.
Hug another person
And the beast may be there.

That kiss of last bravado
Could be the kiss of death
The sweat taste of rebellion
Could be the beast upon your breath.

To fight this unseen creature
That lurks round every street
We must learn to keep our distance
Be calm, be clean, be sweet.

No sword can kill this monster
That takes so many lives
Only we, by working together,
Can save husband's, daughters, sons and wives.

But when this beast is vanquished

From our land
We will look around, breath,
And hopefully finally understand.

We are not the enemy
We are all the same.

Let's hope we all come out if this on the other side.
Not only safer but wiser.

CHRISTMAS IS COMING

Christmas is coming and our leaders are getting fat!

There will be more money in the chancellor's hat.

Will he use it like a Christian and give to the elderly and poor.

My arse he will come New Year he will be asking for more!

TRAVELLERS

Life is like a mystery train journey.

You get on and you don't know where you are going or who you are going to meet.

You meet many different people on the way.

Some you love get off before you and you have to travel alone for a while.

But then someone else gets on and you want to keep travelling.

Eventually you have to get off and leave those you love to travel on.

Leave them with a smile that they met you and the hope that someone else will get on their train and make them feel just like they made you feel.

That's about as good as it gets. And always be kind to your fellow travellers, it's the same train for all of us.

MY ICICLE

I've known it since it was a snowflake,
Falling softly in the night.
But now it's grown and become
A bloody stalactite.

It's dripped for bloody ages
Right outside my own back door
And I have sort of grown to like it
With each drip, a little more.

It look's so clear and beautiful
And I truly have to say
Will there ever be another stalactite
Like this to pass my way?

The thaw will come
The ice will melt
My stalactite will be gone.
And I will thank the weather
That I can 'carry on'

For I can then move forward
With the stalactite behind.
But it's crystal clear free day off
Will remain inside mind.

TOO MUCH IRONY TO DO

I can't come out to play today,
Too much irony to do.
And then put the carpets in the bath,
For a jolly good shampoo.

The plates won't wash themselves you know,
So I throw them in the bin.
And I never buy a lottery ticket,
Because I seldom ever win.

The car won't start without me,
So for it I must be there.
I can't come out to play today,
It really isn't fair.

I must visit the doctor,
To find out if I'm ill,
And even though I'm not unwell,
I still need a little pill.

The papers must be read right through,
Though they're never black and white.
And I wake to remember I've forgot something,
In the middle of the night.

I wish that I had time to do,

PETER JAMES SMITH

More with every day.
But when I look at the clock on the wall,
The Irony gets in my way.

The daffodils were late this year,
I really must have a word.
As for the weather I truly feel,
It's getting quite absurd.

So alas I won't be out to play,
Far, far too much to do.
I've to run around and save the day,
With some sticky tape and some glue.

THE STAR OF THE SHOW

Want to know how to do stuff?

Make an old dress look new?
Bake some biscuits, change a plug fuse or make a stew?
Want to take a piece of wood and turn it into a sword, a magic wand or a rifle?
Make some scones or a sherry trifle?

Want to to have the time of your life and believe you can catch a fish with a stick and a pen knife?
Want to see the flowers and smell the breeze?
Want to scrape the mud off your knees.

Well here's a trick to do all that:
turn off the TV, the mobile, the tablet and all that jazz.

Take the kids, the grand kids or just you.
Pull down that cotton from off the shelf,
dig out the baking tins and the flour and spend an hour by yourself.

Find that old pen knife but find it quick, for life is passing and soon that stick will be brittle and old.

Too soon time passes and we will for sure one day wish that we had done more of the things that matter every day with the people we love.

Enjoy a lager but may your old age memories not be Candy Crush Saga!
Grab every moment and take every chance to dance, laugh and

sing with the people who matter to you, now go.

Don't miss one moment of just who you are because to those that love you, you are the star of their show!

HOLD YOUR HORSES

Steady thy hand.

Young man don't shake so much
For you may make me a feared!

Tomorrow night, at 8pm I will clap the NHS.
As always.
I didn't stop because they didn't.

Too many a marching tune with piper, drums and
Flags a waving pass quickly and easily from the memory.
Emotions are worn down.
The conflict drags on.

How quickly we forget.

The war is not over
Even with a few battles won.
Steady thy hand for the fight
And do not forget those brave souls son.

We clapped and cheered last year.
They are still here and even braver.
This year.
Worn out and tired.
Battle weary and torn.

Steady thy hand and remember most.

We are all in this together!

Stay safe, stay strong and think of those who have worked tirelessly for the last year and have to now carry on.

My fighting days are long since gone
So I can only do what I can.

Steady thy nerves and thy hand for the fight.
Alas the fighting is not done.

Remember young man
A shaking hand makes me shake.

So steady. Steady.

Just hold your horses!

Here comes 2021.

A QUICK RELEASE

The Lockdown's nearly over
The end is nearly come.
I've baked a thousand cookies
And the vaccine's on the run.

My bread making is terrible.
My fairy cakes are stale.
I've drank a million bottles
Of wine and beer and ale.

I've watched every programme
I believe that I can bear.
I've a thousand ways to do a spud
If you could come and and be there.

I've avoided for a whole year
All the things that I should do.
Sadly as it goes
I've also avoided you.

THE NEWS

I've Just read the news.

Don't!

Apparently there is a new more virulent strain of politician than there was before.
And they are mutating at an alarming rate!
They are also breeding beings that do their bidding.

Using new ways to infiltrate your world
Like social media, GPS and their dogs.
Still though people seem to accept it.
Put up with it

Like hogs
In a trough.
While they take away our freedoms.

... away.

Hey.

The survival of a deadly disease
Does not equate to submission.
I don't remember being asked for permission
To live in a police state.

Wait.

Policed by consent!

Policed by consent?

Whos?

THE INTERNET GURU

I've decided to become an interweb superhighway Guru.

Offering advice on many subjects that I know absolutely nothing about.

I'm going to get my own insterweb channel and also a tubeyou one!

If anyone has any concerns about anything they don't understand simply log on to my daily oddcast.

It will hopefully baffle you even more than you are now.

As for live streaming, I love a live stream, ducks and all.

Maybe just switch off
Look and listen to the wonderful world around you.

Take a walk. Find a live stream.

Logging off for now fellow Interweb Superhighway users.

Stay safe

The Guru

A MIRROR

The moment when you wake.
From dreams that make no sense at all.
But.
To you.

Scratch your head, with bleary eyes,
Step out of bed.
The mirror?
The mirror!

Are you still here?

Then you see your eyes.
To no surprise
Only our eyes looking back to see

I looked into a mirror
That looked into a mirror
Which took me to
Infinity.

I dreamed a dream of me dreaming.
Which kept me going
Endlessly.

Everything was smelted.
As the ice flow was melted.
By the warm radiation of the sun.

The people sang,
The people cried,

The people laughed,
And eventually sighed.

Perhaps I imagined my imagination.
Or perhaps,
My imagination imagined me.
Or perhaps,
It simply couldn't be.

So I looked into a mirror,
Which looked into a mirror,
That took me to infinity.

Look closely into that mirror.
And realise that nobody can see you.
As you see you.
To thine own self be true.

I looked into a mirror.

SUNRISE

Today is a beautiful day because
You woke this morning.
Today is a beautiful day because
Someone loves you.

Today is a beautiful day because
You can stare at the clouds and dream.
Today is a beautiful day because
You are alive.

Do not let yesterday spoil your today
Nor let today spoil the unknown tomorrow.
Do not let your tears be afraid to fall
Yet, dwell not so much, on your sorrow.

Do not let fear or worry trouble
The mind that's clear in you.
Do not let anything stop you from doing
What you know and think you will do.

Today is a wonderful creation that often
One can take for granted.
But today is only twenty four hours long
So like the birds sing your song.
Today is a beautiful day

If You Choose to make it that way.
Have a beautiful day citizens and remember
There is a lot of bad out there

BUT

There's a damn site more good.
We win by not being afraid to say,
Hey,
It's a beautiful day xxx

CHANNEL SURFING

There he is, as large as life upon my TV screen,
The man they have in Washington who says he has a dream,
That one day all the world will live in perfect harmony,
And drink down Coca-cola and eat Big Mac's for tea.

His dream, he said, was sure and true and peace was on his mind,
But when they started bombing, he said, peace is hard to find!
He said as how he really didn't like to interfere,
But thought that the world could use some help from the State Department here.

An eagle on his shoulder and a hawk stood by his side,
He said he found his country filled him up with immense pride.
The tanks they just keep rolling and the missiles fire at will,
But everyone is running scared and the children are dying still.

There he is, as large as life upon my TV screen.
The man they have in Russia, who says he has a dream.
That under the ice cap they will find minerals and wealth,
They planted a flag with a submarine, but this is not called stealth.

He's checked the map, the tectonic plates and the cartographer's new view,
And says that other's claims on this are just a load of pooh.
The bankers are talking up money as the Government is talking it down.
The emergency services wait for help as another fellow is

drowned.

Half the world is hungry, the other half is at war

And nobody stops to see what's wrong with the poor laying dead on the floor.

Buy a red nose to change the world, as bonuses go through the roof.

Nobody is being charged at the top as they haven't got any proof.

And there he is, as large as life, upon my TV screen.

The man they have in Downing Street, who says he has a dream.

We're all in this together boys, so get ready to go over the top.

I'll be here in Parliament Square trying to get it all to stop.

Just one more click, it's safe to say, to save my sanity.

The off button, on the bottom of my TV.

Click Off.

citizenpete@yahoo.com

Printed in Great Britain
by Amazon